The BASIC Book
Text copyright © 1985 by Seymour Simon
Illustrations copyright © 1985 by Ed Emberley
Printed in the U.S.A. All rights reserved.
Designed by Al Cetta
1 2 3 4 5 6 7 8 9 10　　　　　First Edition

Library of Congress Cataloging in Publication Data
Simon, Seymour.
　The BASIC book.

　(Let's-read-and-find-out science book)
　Summary: Explains the fundamentals of programming, with simple exercises, in the BASIC language.
　1. Basic (Computer program language)—Juvenile literature. [1. Programming (Computers) 2. Basic (Computer program language)] I. Emberley, Barbara, ill. II. Emberley, Ed, ill. III. Title. IV. Series.
QA76.73.B3S554 1985　　　001.64'24　　　85-47532
ISBN 0-690-04472-0
ISBN 0-690-04473-9 (lib. bdg.)

The *Let's-Read-and-Find-Out Science Book* series was originated by Dr. Franklyn M. Branley, Astronomer Emeritus and former Chairman of The American Museum–Hayden Planetarium, and was formerly co-edited by him and Dr. Roma Gans, Professor Emeritus of Childhood Education, Teachers College, Columbia University. For a complete catalog of Let's-Read-and-Find-Out Science Books, write to Thomas Y. Crowell Junior Books, 10 East 53rd Street, New York, NY 10022.

Other Recent Let's-Read-and-Find-Out Science Books™ You Will Enjoy

Sunshine Makes the Seasons · Bits and Bytes · Hurricane Watch · My Visit to the Dinosaurs · Meet the Computer · Flash, Crash, Rumble, and Roll · Volcanoes · Dinosaurs Are Different · Germs Make Me Sick! · What Happens to a Hamburger · How to Talk to Your Computer · Comets · Rock Collecting · Is There Life in Outer Space? · All Kinds of Feet · Flying Giants of Long Ago · Rain and Hail · Why I Cough, Sneeze, Shiver, Hiccup, & Yawn · You Can't Make a Move Without Your Muscles · The Sky Is Full of Stars · The Planets in Our Solar System · Digging Up Dinosaurs · No Measles, No Mumps for Me · When Birds Change Their Feathers · Birds Are Flying · A Jellyfish Is Not a Fish · Cactus in the Desert · Me and My Family Tree · Redwoods Are the Tallest Trees in the World · Shells Are Skeletons · Caves · Wild and Woolly Mammoths · The March of the Lemmings · Corals · Energy from the Sun · Corn Is Maize · The Eel's Strange Journey

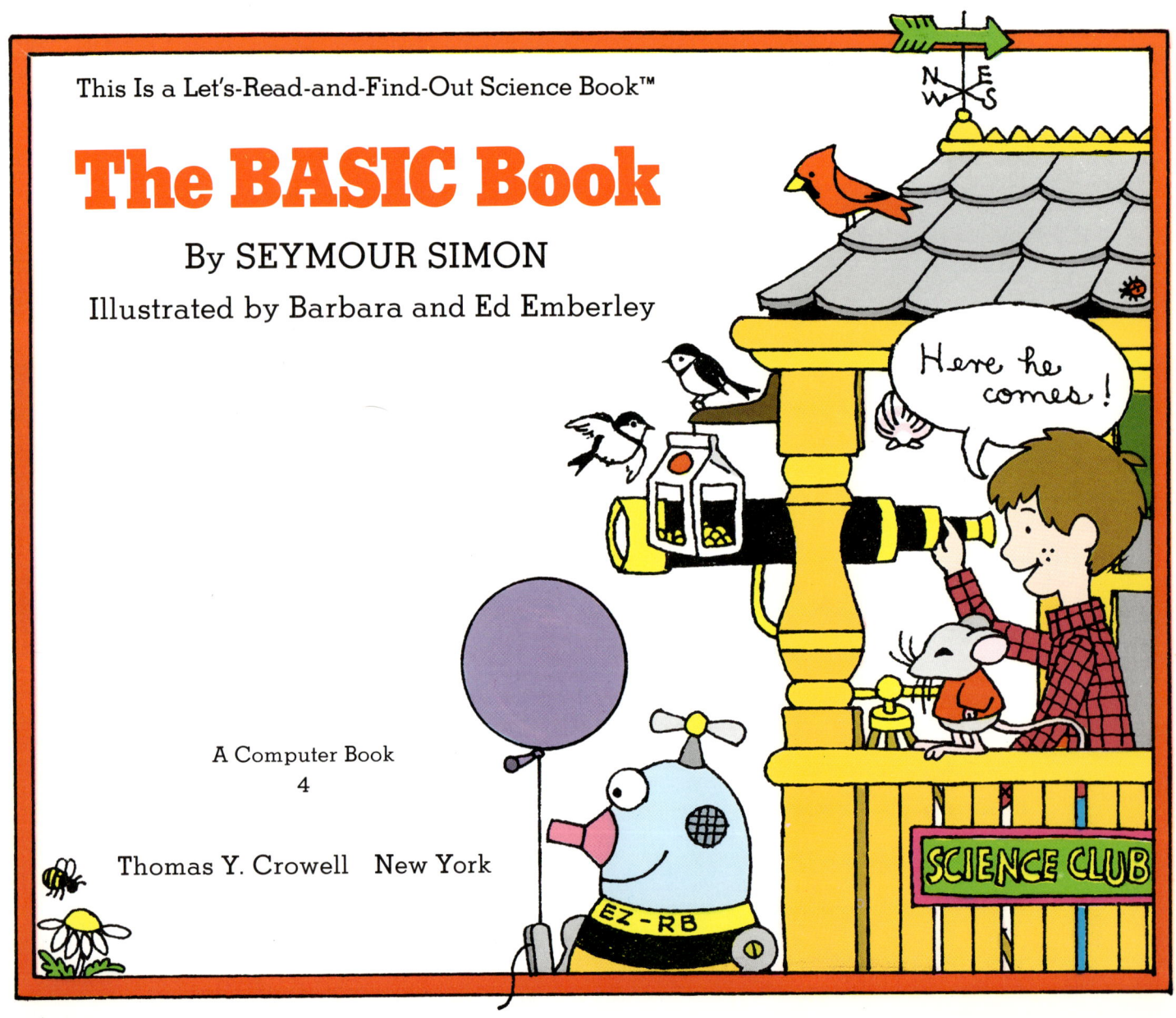

The BASIC Book

You want to tell the computer to wish Adam a happy birthday. But you can't just speak to a home computer and tell it what you want. It won't understand.

A computer will do what you want only if you give it exact, step-by-step instructions.

A step-by-step list of instructions for a computer to follow is called a **program**.

Programs have to be written in a "language" computers understand.

There are many different computer languages. BASIC is one language most home computers understand.

```
NEW
10 PRINT "HELLO, ADAM."
20 PRINT "HAPPY BIRTHDAY!"
30 END
```

```
NEW
10 PRINT "HELLO, ADAM."
20 PRINT "HAPPY BIRTHDAY!"
30 END
```

Here is a BASIC program to wish Adam a happy birthday.

Every step in a BASIC program is called a **statement**. The statements tell the computer what to do.

```
NEW
10 PRINT "HELLO, ADAM."
20 PRINT "HAPPY BIRTHDAY!"
30 END
```

"3 line numbers."

```
        NEW
FIRST   10 PRINT "HELLO, ADAM."
SECOND  20 PRINT "HAPPY BIRTHDAY!"
THIRD   30 END

        NEW
THIRD   30 END
FIRST   10 PRINT "HELLO, ADAM."
SECOND  20 PRINT "HAPPY BIRTHDAY!"
```

Every statement in a BASIC program has a **line number**.

The computer follows the line numbers to do things in order. It goes to the lowest line number first. Then it goes to the next lowest line number, and so on.

You can even mix the numbers up. The computer will still follow them in order.

```
NEW
10 PRINT "HELLO, ADAM."
20 PRINT "HAPPY BIRTHDAY!"
30 END
```

```
NEW
10 PRINT "HELLO, ADAM."
20 PRINT "HAPPY BIRTHDAY!"
30 END
```

This program has 3 different command words.

Every statement in a BASIC program begins with a special **command word**

NEW is a command word in BASIC. The word **NEW** at the beginning of a program tells the computer to forget all the other programs you gave it.

NEW always comes first, and it doesn't need a line number.

PRINT is another command word. It tells the computer to print everything between the quotation marks.

END tells the computer to stop doing the program.

You can give a computer a program by typing it on the computer's keyboard.

At the end of each statement you press the special key marked **RETURN**.

(On some keyboards this key is marked **ENTER**.)

Type this statement.	NEW	Then press RETURN.
Type this statement.	10 PRINT "HELLO, ADAM."	Then press RETURN.
Type this statement.	20 PRINT "HAPPY BIRTHDAY!"	Then press RETURN.
Type this statement.	30 END	Then press RETURN.

"Now the whole program is entered."

After you enter the program, you want to check how it works. Type the word **RUN** and press the **RETURN** key.

```
NEW
10 PRINT "HELLO, ADAM."
20 PRINT "HAPPY BIRTHDAY!"
30 END

RUN
HELLO, ADAM.
HAPPY BIRTHDAY!
```

Here's what the computer shows on the screen.

You can change the program whenever you like. First, call back the program to the screen by typing the word LIST and pressing the RETURN key.

THIS IS WHAT SHOWS ON THE SCREEN.

LIST
10 PRINT "HELLO, ADAM."
20 PRINT "HAPPY BIRTHDAY!"
30 END

Suppose you want to add a statement. Type this on the computer keyboard.

15 PRINT "ALL YOUR FRIENDS WISH YOU A"

Don't forget to press RETURN at the end of the statement.

HERE'S THE PROGRAM YOU NOW SEE ON THE SCREEN.

You did it!

LIST
10 PRINT "HELLO, ADAM."
20 PRINT "HAPPY BIRTHDAY!"
30 END
15 PRINT "ALL YOUR FRIENDS WISH YOU A"

Now the surprise birthday program for Adam is ready. And here comes Adam.

You tell him to type **RUN** and press the **RETURN** key.

Here is what comes on the screen.

```
RUN
HELLO, ADAM.
ALL YOUR FRIENDS WISH YOU A
HAPPY BIRTHDAY!
■
```

The computer followed the line numbers in order. That's why it printed line 15 after line 10 and before line 20.

It's a good idea to number program lines by fives or tens when you write a program. That way you can always add some new lines in between.

You can change a line, too. Just type the line number again and then the new statement.

First, type LIST and press the RETURN key to call back the program to the screen.

Then type this line on the keyboard.

15 PRINT "ALL OF US WISH YOU A VERY"

Now type RUN and press RETURN.

Here's what comes on the screen.

```
LIST
10 PRINT "HELLO, ADAM."
15 PRINT "ALL YOUR FRIENDS WISH YOU A"
20 PRINT "HAPPY BIRTHDAY!"
30 END
■
```

```
RUN
HELLO, ADAM.
ALL OF US WISH YOU A VERY
HAPPY BIRTHDAY!
■
```

You can get rid of a statement completely by typing the line number and pressing the **RETURN** key.

Type 15 and press the **RETURN** key.

What do you think you will see when you **RUN** the program?

I'd like to try that one.

That looks easy.

```
RUN
HELLO, ADAM.
HAPPY BIRTHDAY!
```

That's not all you can do with the computer.

Here's how you can make the computer skip a line in the program. You use the command word, **GOTO**.

Type this program on the keyboard.

```
NEW
10  PRINT "LET'S SKIP A LINE."
20  GOTO 40
30  PRINT "WHERE HAVE I GONE?"
40  PRINT "LINE 30 IS HIDING."
50  END
```

Type the word **RUN** and press the **RETURN** key.

Here is what comes on the screen.

```
RUN
LET'S SKIP A LINE.
LINE 30 IS HIDING.
■
```

GOTO is a BASIC command word made up of the words "go" and "to."

The statement in line 20

told the computer to go to line 40 directly.

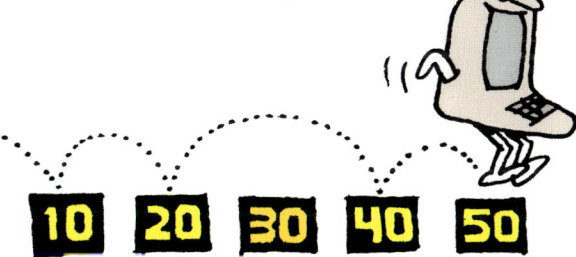

That means the computer skipped over line 30.

You can also make the computer repeat a line. It can repeat the same line as many times as you want. All you have to do is use the FOR...NEXT commands.

Type this program into the computer.

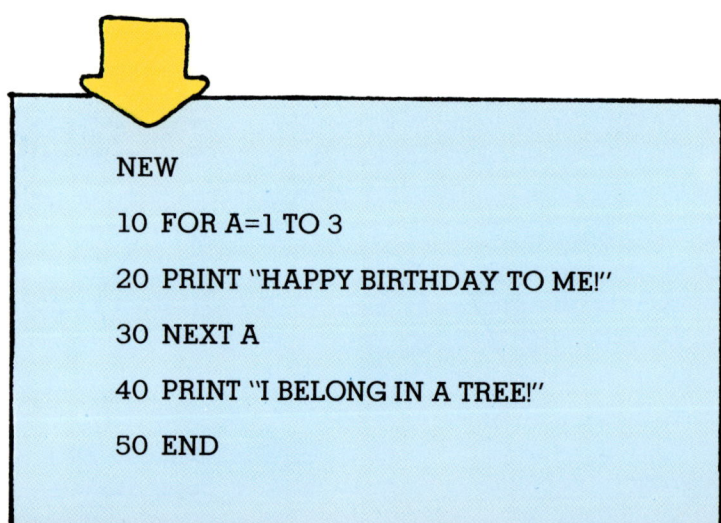

```
NEW
10  FOR A=1 TO 3
20  PRINT "HAPPY BIRTHDAY TO ME!"
30  NEXT A
40  PRINT "I BELONG IN A TREE!"
50  END
```

The computer went in a circle called a **loop**. The loop in the program you used is called a **FOR...NEXT** loop.

The statement that begins with the command word FOR tells the computer exactly how many times to do something.

```
NEW
10 FOR A=1 TO 3
20 PRINT "HAPPY BIRTHDAY TO ME!"
30 NEXT A
40 PRINT "I BELONG IN A TREE!"
50 END
```

10 FOR A= 1 TO 3
20 PRINT "HAPPY BIRTHDAY TO ME!"

THE COMPUTER USES THIS STATEMENT TO KEEP COUNT.

THIS NUMBER SAYS HOW MANY.

NEXT tells the computer to go back to **A** on line 10.

After the computer goes back the exact number of times you told it to, it goes on to the rest of the program.

10 FOR A= 1 TO 3
20 PRINT "HAPPY BIRTHDAY TO ME!"
30 NEXT A

NEW
10 FOR A=1 TO 3
20 PRINT "HAPPY BIRTHDAY TO ME!"
30 NEXT A
40 PRINT "I BELONG IN A TREE!"
50 END

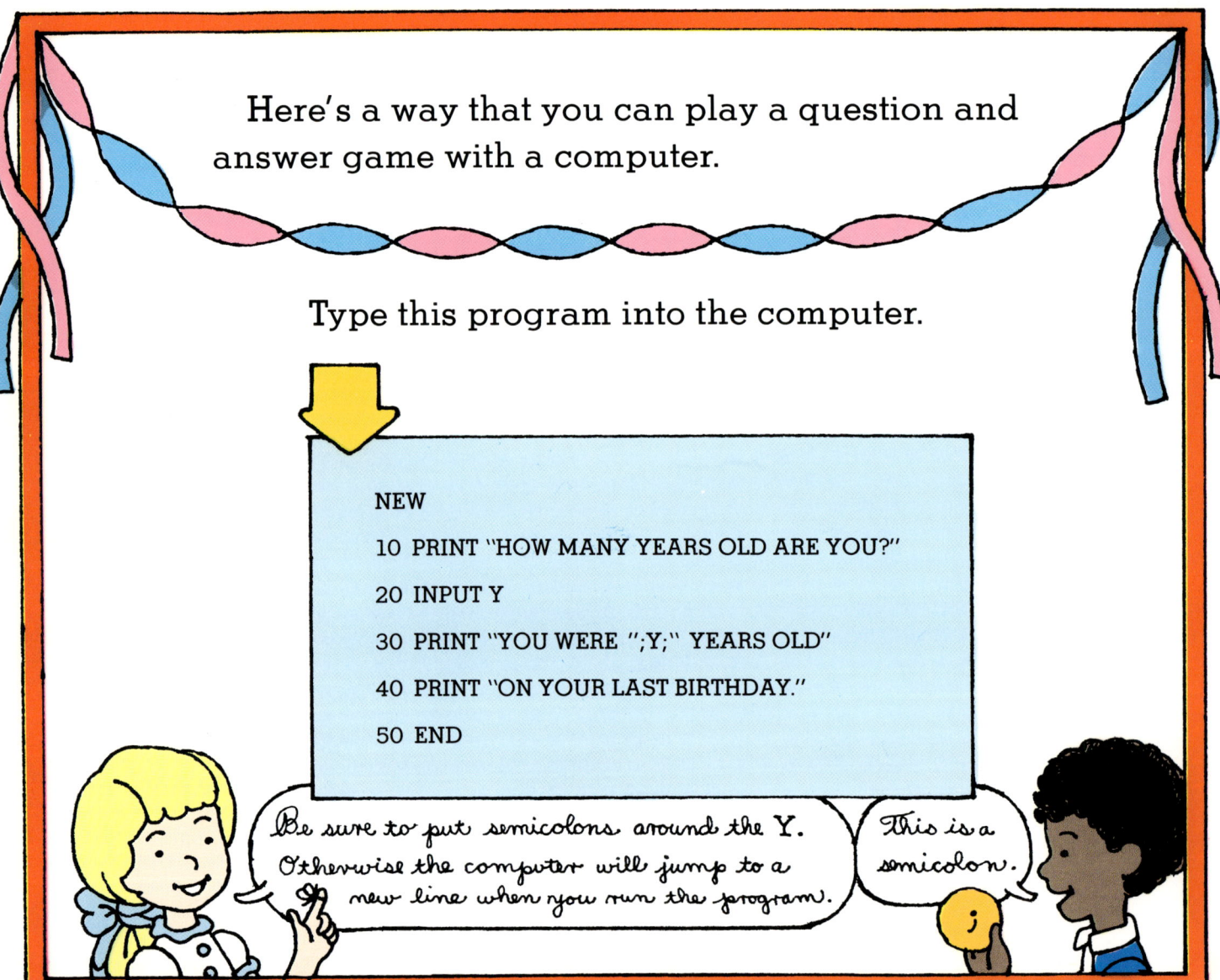

Type the word **RUN** and press the **RETURN** key.

```
RUN
HOW MANY YEARS OLD ARE YOU?
? ▪
```

Suppose you type the number 7.

```
RUN
HOW MANY YEARS OLD ARE YOU?
?7 ▪
```

When you press the **RETURN** key the screen will show this.

```
RUN
HOW MANY YEARS OLD ARE YOU?
?7
YOU WERE 7 YEARS OLD
ON YOUR LAST BIRTHDAY.
▪
```

The computer may seem to be talking to you. But it is really not that smart.

You made the computer print a question with line 10.

Then the command word **INPUT** in line 20 made the computer print a question mark and wait for your answer.

You typed in a number.

Then the computer put that number in place of the Y in line 30.

Every time someone runs the program, he or she can put in a different number.

```
NEW
10 PRINT "HOW MANY YEARS OLD ARE YOU?"
20 INPUT Y
30 PRINT "YOU WERE ";Y;" YEARS OLD"
40 PRINT "ON YOUR LAST BIRTHDAY."
50 END
■
RUN
HOW MANY YEARS OLD ARE YOU?
?■
RUN
HOW MANY YEARS OLD ARE YOU?
?7■
RUN
HOW MANY YEARS OLD ARE YOU?
?7
YOU WERE 7 YEARS OLD
ON YOUR LAST BIRTHDAY.
■
RUN
HOW MANY YEARS OLD ARE YOU?
? 700
YOU WERE 700 YEARS OLD
ON YOUR LAST BIRTHDAY.
■
```

"Now I want to write a program for all my friends," Adam says.

He types this on the computer keyboard.

```
NEW
10  PRINT "HELLO, EVERYONE!"
20  PRINT "THIS IS YOUR FRIEND ADAM"
30  PRINT "MAKING A COMPUTER TELL YOU"
40  PRINT "SOMETHING IMPORTANT."
50  PRINT "WHAT A GREAT BIRTHDAY!"
60  FOR A=1 TO 8
70  PRINT "THANK YOU!"
80  NEXT A
90  PRINT "THAT'S ONE THANK YOU"
100 PRINT "FOR EACH FRIEND."
110 END
```

Then Adam types RUN and presses the RETURN key. What do you think everyone sees on the screen?

RUN

HELLO, EVERYONE!

THIS IS YOUR FRIEND ADAM

MAKING A COMPUTER TELL YOU

SOMETHING IMPORTANT.

WHAT A GREAT BIRTHDAY!

THANK YOU!

THANK YOU!

THANK YOU!

THANK YOU!

THANK YOU!

THANK YOU!

THANK YOU!

THANK YOU!

THAT'S ONE THANK YOU

FOR EACH FRIEND.

■

Dictionary of BASIC Words

BASIC A computer language that lets you "talk" to your computer using English words. BASIC stands for <u>B</u>eginner's <u>A</u>ll-purpose <u>S</u>ymbolic <u>I</u>nstruction <u>C</u>ode.

COMMAND WORD An order to the computer telling it what to do.

END The last word in a BASIC program. It tells the computer to stop doing the program. Some computers do not need an END command.

FOR...NEXT A command in BASIC that tells a computer to do something a certain number of times.

GOTO A word in BASIC that tells the computer to go to a different place in the program. GOTO is always followed by a line number.

INPUT A word in BASIC that tells the computer to wait for some information before it does anything else.

LINE NUMBER A number at the beginning of a statement in a BASIC program.

LIST A BASIC command that tells a computer to show all the statements in a program in number order.

LOOP A part of a program that makes a computer do something over again a number of times.

NEW A word in BASIC that tells a computer to clear out any old programs in its memory.

PRINT A word in BASIC that tells a computer to show something on the screen.

PROGRAM A list of instructions for a computer to do.

RETURN or **ENTER** A key on a computer keyboard that you press after you type something. The computer will not do anything with a line you type until you press the RETURN key.

RUN A BASIC command that tells a computer to start doing a program.

SEMICOLON (;) A semicolon outside quotation marks tells the computer to stay where it is and not begin a new line.

STATEMENT A line of instructions in a computer program.